THE LEGEND AND MYTHS OF HAWAII

Unveiling Ancient Stories of Gods, Heroes, and Sacred Traditions That Shaped the Aloha Spirit

By

LUKE STRICKLAND

PREFACE

"The stories never die. They drift on the wind, waiting for ears that will listen."

There is a power in myths—a force that shapes the soul of a people, whispers through the generations, and lingers in the land itself. In Hawaii, these stories are not just tales told around a fire; they are woven into the very fabric of existence. They are the voice of the mountains, the breath of the ocean, and the unseen footsteps that walk the earth long after mortal feet have faded.

To outsiders, Hawaii is often seen as a paradise of turquoise waters, golden sands, and gentle breezes. But to those who listen closely, this land holds something far more profound. It holds echoes of the gods, the footsteps of warriors who march even in death, and the remnants of a world where the divine and the human walked side by side.

The legends and myths of Hawaii are more than stories. They are truths disguised as fables, histories whispered through generations, and warnings carved into the bones of the land. They tell of Pele, the fiery goddess who shapes and destroys with equal fury. Of Maui, the trickster who defied the heavens and stole time itself. Of the Night Marchers, whose presence still chills the air of sacred valleys, reminding us that the past is never truly gone.

But these stories are not frozen in time. They live. They breathe. They change.

Hawaii's history has been one of triumph and loss, of reverence and erasure. The gods were once honored in sacred heiaus, their names chanted beneath the stars. But with time came change—first the fall of the kapu system, then the arrival of missionaries, and later, the suppression of Hawaiian language and culture. Myths that once defined a people were pushed to the margins, whispered only in secret.

Yet legends do not die so easily.

In the 20th century, a cultural awakening surged through the islands—the Hawaiian Renaissance. It was a reclamation, a remembering. The stories of old were given new breath, hula was danced with renewed purpose, and the voices of ancestors were no longer silenced.

Today, these myths are more than relics; they are the heartbeat of a people. They remind us that Hawaii is not just a place but a living story—one that continues to be written with each passing tide.

This book is not just a collection of tales; it is a journey. A journey into a world where the gods still whisper through the waves, where ancient spirits still walk the land, and where legends remain as alive as the people who tell them.

As you turn these pages, may you not just read these stories—may you feel them. May they stir something deep within you, something primal, something eternal.

For the legends of Hawaii are not just history. They are a voice calling across time, waiting for ears that will listen.

And now, the story begins.

Table Of Contents

- Table Of Contents — 5
- 1 — 7
- The Birth of the Hawaiian Islands – A Myth Forged in Fire — 7
- 2 — 15
- MAUI – THE TRICKSTER WHO STOLE THE SUN — 15
- 3 — 24
- THE NIGHT MARCHERS – WHEN THE DEAD WALK THE EARTH — 24
- 4 — 33
- THE MENEHUNE – BUILDERS OF THE IMPOSSIBLE — 33
- 5 — 40
- LOVE, BETRAYAL, AND THE WRATH OF THE GODS — 40
- 6 — 47
- THE MOʻO – GUARDIANS OF WATER AND SHADOW — 47
- 7 — 55
- THE FALL OF THE KAPU SYSTEM – WHEN GODS WERE SILENCED — 55
- 8 — 65
- THE CURSE OF KAMEHAMEHA'S BONES — 65
- 9 — 74
- THE HAWAIIAN RENAISSANCE – RECLAIMING LOST STORIES — 74

10
THE TIMELESS ECHO OF LEGENDS 84 84

1

The Birth of the Hawaiian Islands – A Myth Forged in Fire

"From the depths of the ocean rose the islands, sculpted by fire, shaped by fury, and blessed by the goddess who walks among the flames."

The arrival of pele – a goddess in search of home

The night sky over the Pacific was endless—an infinite stretch of black silk, punctuated only by the flickering glow of distant stars. Beneath this celestial expanse, a solitary canoe sliced through the waves, its occupant aflame with destiny.

Pele had been cast out.

The fire goddess, the one who carried the rage of creation within her, had been driven from her homeland in Kahiki. She had defied the balance of gods, her ambition too fierce, her power too uncontrollable. And so, she fled. With each stroke of her paddle, the ocean hissed beneath her touch. Embers flickered in her wake, and the night sky, once serene, bore witness to the arrival of a force that would reshape the world.

The legend tells that Pele sought a home—a place where her fire could burn undisturbed, where her power would not be extinguished by the tides of her jealous sister, Namaka, the goddess of the sea. Island after island she attempted to claim, but Namaka, relentless and unforgiving, pursued her, drowning each fiery foothold before it could take root.

Then, at last, she reached a place where her sister's fury could not follow.

Hawaiʻi.

On the slopes of Kīlauea, Pele found sanctuary. Here, beneath the earth, she carved her fiery domain, birthing a land of molten rock and rising stone. The volcano became her heart, the lava her blood. She sculpted the land with passion and destruction, breathing islands into existence, only to consume them again with her endless hunger. This was her cycle—creation and destruction, birth and death, beauty and devastation, forever intertwined.

But Pele's fire was not merely an act of rage. It was a declaration of life.

A BATTLE OF FIRE AND WATER – THE SHAPING OF THE ISLANDS

The ocean roared in defiance. Namaka had found her.

From the horizon, waves the size of mountains surged toward Pele's sanctuary. The sea goddess, determined to extinguish her sister's flames, unleashed her fury upon the land. The battle that followed was one of legend—the sky darkened with ash, lightning split the heavens, and the earth trembled beneath the weight of gods at war.

Lava and seawater collided, sending towers of steam into the sky, hissing and screaming like wounded spirits. Pele's molten rivers raced toward the ocean, turning water into fire, rock into land. Every time Namaka attempted to drown Pele's work, the fire goddess erupted anew, more powerful, more determined.

And so, the islands were born—not in peace, but in battle.

Hawaiian legend tells us that each of the islands carries the scars of this war. The jagged cliffs, the volcanic craters, the black sand beaches—they are remnants of Pele's defiance, evidence of her triumph over the sea. Even now, she still fights. The lava that flows from Kīlauea is her breath, the eruptions her heartbeat. She is never truly at rest.

Her spirit lingers in the molten rivers that carve new land from the ocean, in the glow of the lava lake that pulses beneath Halemaʻumaʻu Crater. And when the earth shakes, when the sky glows red in the night, the people of Hawaiʻi do not see destruction.

They see Pele, alive and eternal.

THE SCIENCE BEHIND THE MYTH – THE TRUTH IN THE FIRE

Though Pele's legend speaks of divine hands shaping the land, modern science tells its own story—one equally remarkable. The Hawaiian Islands were indeed born of fire, sculpted not by gods, but by the relentless force of the Earth itself.

Deep beneath the Pacific, a geological phenomenon known as a hot spot created the islands over millions of years. Unlike the shifting plates of the Earth's crust, this hot spot remains fixed, a vent of molten rock rising from the mantle. As the Pacific Plate drifts northwest, the hot spot continuously erupts, forming volcanic islands one after another. The youngest, Hawaiʻi Island, still sits above this inferno, while the older islands slowly erode, drifting into the sea.

It is a cycle as old as time. New land is born, old land fades, and the process begins again—an eternal dance of creation and destruction.

The battle between Pele and Namaka, then, is not merely myth. It is a poetic retelling of geological truth. The tension between fire and water, the struggle for dominance between land and sea—this is the reality of the Hawaiian archipelago.

Yet, what science explains with plate tectonics and magma chambers, legend captures with emotion, passion, and soul.

Both tell the truth. One in fact, the other in feeling.

PELE'S PRESENCE IN MODERN HAWAII – A GODDESS WHO ENDURES

Even in the modern age, Pele's presence is undeniable.

For the people of Hawaiʻi, she is not just a myth from the past. She is alive in the land, in the smoke that rises from the craters, in the molten rivers that flow through the night. Her spirit is honored with offerings of ʻōhelo berries and pandanus leaves, left at the rim of Halemaʻumaʻu Crater. Her name is spoken with reverence, her stories passed down through generations.

And those who do not respect her... they learn.

Tales abound of those who took Pele's lava rocks as souvenirs, only to be met with misfortune until they returned them. Tourists send back thousands of rocks to Hawaiʻi each year, fearful of the goddess's curse. Whether by coincidence or divine punishment, those who cross Pele do so at their own peril.

She is in the chants of the hula, the sacred dance that tells her story. She is in the murals that adorn island walls, her image fierce and unyielding. And when Kīlauea erupts, people do not see catastrophe. They see Pele at work, reshaping the land, continuing the cycle she began so long ago.

She is destruction. She is creation. She is the spirit of Hawaiʻi itself.

THE ETERNAL FIRE – PELE'S LEGACY

The story of Pele is not just a legend of the past. It is a story still being written.

Every time lava meets the sea, every time the earth shakes and the sky glows red, her presence is undeniable. She is a reminder that the land we walk upon is alive, that nothing is permanent, and that creation often comes with fire.

Hawai'i is not just a place of beauty; it is a place of power, of transformation, of gods who still walk among mortals. Pele's fire is not a thing of the past. It is a living force, shaping the islands and those who call them home.

And as long as the volcanoes breathe, as long as the land rises from the depths, Pele's legend will never die.

She is the fire that forges the world anew.

She is the goddess who never rests.

She is Hawai'i.

CLOSING THOUGHT

"Some say myths are just stories. But in Hawaii, myths are truths wrapped in fire and stone, whispered by the earth itself. And Pele's story? It is far from over."

2

MAUI – THE TRICKSTER WHO STOLE THE SUN

"The sky burned gold, the mountains cast long shadows, and time itself trembled in the hands of a single demigod."

The challenge of time – a world in shadow

Long ago, before the islands knew balance, before the rhythm of day and night was set, the world suffered under the tyranny of the sun.

It raced across the sky, a blazing orb of fire, indifferent to the struggles of those who lived below. Days were too short. The people of Hawaiʻi—fishermen, farmers, artisans—worked in haste, their labors undone by the swift descent of night. Their crops withered, struggling to soak in the brief hours of light. Their fishnets were barely cast before the ocean turned dark. There was no time.

And so, they called upon Maui.

Maui, the trickster, the demigod, the one who defied gods and reshaped the world. He had already fished up islands, woven wonders from mischief, and now, the people pleaded for his cunning once more.

Could he slow the sun?

Maui listened. His mother, Hina, whose kapa cloth could not dry in the fleeting light, begged him to take action. The elders warned that without change, their way of life would suffer. Even the mountains, standing in solemn patience, seemed to watch, waiting for his answer.

Maui grinned.

"Then I will do it," he declared. *"I will snare the sun and teach it to listen."*

The sky itself seemed to shudder at his words.

A BATTLE AGAINST THE HEAVENS – MAUI'S PLAN

Maui was not a god of patience. He was a god of boldness, of fire and force. He did not plead with the sun—he planned to take it.

Forging a mighty rope from strands of his mother's long hair, braided with fiber from the strongest hala trees, he crafted a snare worthy of the heavens. He traveled to the summit of Haleakalā, the "House of the Sun," where the world touched the sky, where the sun's first breath painted the earth in gold.

There, he waited.

The moment came.

The first light of dawn crested the horizon, illuminating Maui's silhouette against the crimson sky. He crouched, muscles coiled like a predator, his rope gripped tight. The sun rose, swift and merciless, eager to continue its reckless journey across the sky.

Maui lunged.

The rope snapped forward, encircling the sun's fiery limbs. The sky erupted in light. The heat was unbearable, searing his skin, but Maui held fast. The sun thrashed, furious at this defiance. It blazed hotter, the air shimmering with its rage. The mountains trembled, the ocean recoiled, and even the gods turned their gaze toward the battle raging atop Haleakalā.

But Maui would not let go.

He dug his heels into the mountain's peak, straining against the burning force. The battle was relentless—fire against flesh, eternity against mortality. But Maui was relentless too. With every ounce of strength, he tightened the rope, pulling, commanding, demanding.

And the sun... slowed.

Time stretched. Shadows grew long. The day lingered. The people of Hawai'i, far below, watched in awe as the golden light held its place in the sky.

Maui had done the impossible.

The sun, panting, humbled, conceded. *"Release me,"* it pleaded, *"and I will give you what you ask."*

Maui, ever the trickster, smiled. "Then promise me this—no longer shall you race across the heavens unchecked. You will move slowly in summer, granting my people long days to tend their land, and only in winter shall you regain your swiftness."

The sun, exhausted, agreed.

And so, balance was restored. The land flourished, the people thrived, and Maui's legend burned brighter than ever.

THE MEANING BEHIND THE MYTH – A PEOPLE WHO MEASURED THE SKY

At first glance, Maui's tale is one of magic and rebellion, a trickster taming the wild forces of nature. But beneath the story lies something deeper—a reflection of the ancient Hawaiians' profound understanding of the world around them.

Hawaiian society was not one of chaos, but of careful observation. They knew the sun's patterns, understood the shifting length of days, and recognized the changes in the seasons. The myth of Maui slowing the sun was not just a story—it was a mnemonic, a way to remember the natural rhythms that dictated their survival.

The Hawaiians tracked the sun's path across the sky, noting the solstices and equinoxes with precision. They built heiau (sacred temples) aligned with celestial events, ensuring their agricultural cycles remained in harmony with the heavens. They did not need modern science to tell them that daylight was longer in summer, shorter in winter—they had Maui's tale to explain it.

And what better way to remember the sun's behavior than with a story of a rogue demigod, a battle atop the mountains, and a trick that forever changed time itself?

The myth was science. The science was myth.

And together, they formed a truth more powerful than either alone.

THE TRICKSTER'S LEGACY – MAUI'S PRESENCE IN MODERN HAWAI'I

Today, Maui's legend is more than just a tale of the past. His spirit endures, woven into the identity of the Hawaiian people.

His name is spoken with pride, carved into the land itself—the island of Maui, a tribute to the demigod who shaped the world. His story is immortalized in hula, in chants, in the oral traditions passed from one generation to the next.

Artists paint him, his lasso raised against the fiery sun. Storytellers invoke his mischief, reminding listeners that wit and courage can bend even the laws of the universe. And in the mountains, where the first light of dawn kisses Haleakalā, visitors still whisper his name, as if expecting to see his shadow against the horizon.

But his greatest legacy?

It is in the people who continue to defy limits. The surfers who ride the impossible waves. The voyagers who sail by the stars, reviving the lost art of wayfinding.

The activists who fight to preserve their land, their language, their traditions.

Maui is more than a myth.

He is a reminder that the world is not fixed, that rules can be rewritten, that even the sun itself can be challenged.

And that, sometimes, all it takes is a rope, a trick, and the will to change the course of history.

THE ETERNAL TRICKSTER – THE STORY THAT NEVER ENDS

Maui's tale is not bound by time.

It is told in the flicker of firelight, in the laughter of children who dream of catching the sun. It is in the hearts of those who refuse to accept the impossible, who believe that even the heavens can be reshaped with enough wit and determination.

The sun still moves, but it does so at Maui's pace.

The world still turns, but it carries his story forward.

And as long as there are those who dare to defy, who challenge, who create, Maui will live on.

He is not just a legend.

He is Hawaiʻi.

CLOSING THOUGHT

"The sun once ran wild, untamed and relentless. But then came Maui, the trickster, the rebel, the one who knew that even the brightest forces could be outwitted. And the world, forever changed, still carries his mark in every lingering sunset."

3

THE NIGHT MARCHERS – WHEN THE DEAD WALK THE EARTH

"The drums begin at night, deep and resonant, like the heartbeat of something ancient. The air thickens. The wind stills. And then, in the distance, torches flicker in an unbroken line, moving with a purpose that does not belong to the living."

A warning in the wind – the traveler's nightmare

The jungle whispered, its leaves stirring in unseen currents. The night was thick, swollen with humidity, the scent of damp earth and salt drifting up from the sea.

Kaleo adjusted his backpack, his steps careful as he navigated the overgrown trail. He had heard the stories before—warnings murmured by locals who refused to set foot here after dark. The valley was sacred. The dead still walked.

He hadn't believed them.

Now, standing beneath the looming cliffs of Kaʻawa Valley, the weight of the night pressing down on him, doubt crept in.

Then, the first sound came.

A low, distant thump.

A drumbeat.

Kaleo froze. His breath caught in his throat. It came again—deeper, closer. The earth trembled beneath his feet, the vibrations crawling up his spine.

The air changed.

The soft rustle of wind died. The chirping insects fell silent. Even the trees, swaying moments ago, now stood unnaturally still.

A cold shiver wrapped around him.

He turned.

Down the valley, where the mist curled thick over the land, torches appeared. They flickered, golden-red against the night, moving in a slow, unyielding line. Shadows stretched long across the grass, figures materializing between the flames—tall, armored warriors marching in perfect silence.

The Night Marchers.

Panic clawed at Kaleo's chest. He knew what he had to do.

Drop to the ground. Face down. Do not look. Do not move.

The old warnings rang in his ears. Those who meet the eyes of the Night Marchers do not live to tell of it.

He fell to his knees, pressing his forehead into the earth.

The drums grew louder. The air thickened, charged with something beyond human understanding.

And then—feet.

Bare and calloused, stepping in perfect rhythm past his trembling body. The scent of ti leaves and sweat, the metallic tang of ancient weapons. Voices murmuring in a language older than the wind.

The march continued, unstoppable. The dead did not pause.

And then—silence.

Kaleo dared not move. Minutes passed, maybe hours. When he finally looked up, the torches were gone. The mist had lifted. The jungle breathed again.

He was alone.

But the ground beneath him was still warm, as if something—someone—had just passed through.

SPIRITS OF THE PAST – THE ORIGINS OF THE NIGHT MARCHERS

The legend of the Night Marchers (huaka'i pō) is not a simple ghost story. It is a thread woven deep into the history of Hawaii, tied to the sacred rituals of a time long past.

Before Western contact, Hawaii was a land of strict kapu (taboos) and deeply held spiritual beliefs. The ali'i (chiefs) ruled with divine authority, and the highest-ranking among them were so sacred that commoners were forbidden to look upon them. When these chiefs traveled, warriors marched ahead in solemn processions, beating drums, blowing conch shells, and carrying torches to clear the path.

Those who failed to show proper respect—who stood in the way, who dared to meet the chief's gaze—were executed on the spot.

Even in death, it is said, these processions continue. The spirits of warriors and chiefs march as they did in life, bound to their duty, unable to rest.

Their paths are known: the cliffs of Nuʻuanu, the valleys of Oʻahu, the lava fields of the Big Island. Sacred sites, places of power.

And when the drums sound in the night, even the bravest know to step aside.

WHISPERS IN THE DARK – MODERN ENCOUNTERS

The stories have not faded with time.

Ask a local, and they will tell you: the Night Marchers are real.

There are those who have seen the torches flickering along ridges, moving with unnatural precision. Hikers who have felt the air shift, the sudden silence swallowing all sound before the distant beat of drums begins. Security guards at remote resorts who have watched, frozen, as shadowy figures pass through walls, their forms illuminated by phantom fire.

One story, often told, is of a construction worker on the Big Island. He was digging on sacred land when the wind turned cold. The air crackled with unseen energy.

That night, he woke to the sound of conch shells outside his tent. When he stepped out, he saw them—warriors in feathered cloaks, torches reflecting in their hollow eyes. He collapsed to his knees, whispering prayers, and when he looked again, they were gone.

The next morning, the ground where they had stood was scorched.

Even today, locals take precautions. Houses built near known Night Marcher trails have doors on both sides—an escape route should the spirits come. Some hang ti leaves around their homes, a sacred plant said to ward off restless spirits. And many, no matter how skeptical, refuse to challenge the old beliefs.

Because in Hawaii, the past is never truly gone.

THE VEIL BETWEEN WORLDS – MYTH AND REALITY

What separates myth from history?

The Night Marchers are not ghosts in the Western sense. They are not lost souls, nor malevolent phantoms seeking revenge. They are guardians, keepers of the old ways, a reminder that Hawaii is a land where the past still walks alongside the present.

Perhaps the stories persist because they hold a deeper truth—one not bound by logic, but by the weight of history itself.

The Night Marchers are more than legend.

They are Hawaii's memory.

And when the drums sound, when the torches glow, when the wind stills and the air hums with something beyond this world, those who listen carefully will understand:

The dead are never far away.

THE FINAL ECHO – A HAUNTING REFLECTION

Somewhere in the valleys, the march continues.

Somewhere in the night, the drums still sound.

And somewhere, even now, a traveler walks a path they should not tread, unaware that the air has changed, that the leaves have stilled, that the unseen gaze of ancient warriors has fallen upon them.

They do not yet hear the beat of the drums.

But they will.

And when they do—

They will know they are not alone.

CLOSING THOUGHT

"The past is not buried beneath the earth. It marches. It watches. And when the time is right, it reminds us that history does not sleep—it walks beside us in the dark."

4

THE MENEHUNE – BUILDERS OF THE IMPOSSIBLE

"Under the cloak of night, they work—small hands shaping the impossible, stones moving in silence, an entire world built before the first light of dawn. And then, as suddenly as they appeared, they are gone, leaving behind only the wonder of what was created."

The night of the builders – a menehune miracle

The stars burned bright over Kauaʻi, their light shimmering on the calm waters of the river. In the stillness of the night, not a single voice rose, not a single footstep echoed. But something was happening.

Deep in the valley, tiny figures moved in perfect synchrony. The Menehune had come.

They were no taller than a child, their bodies quick and sturdy, their hands roughened by the shaping of stone and wood. They worked in silence, their eyes glinting in the moonlight as they passed massive stones down the line, each one fitting seamlessly into place.

Tonight, their task was great.

The chief of the valley had wished for a loko i'a, a fishpond strong enough to sustain his people. But the work was impossible for mortal hands alone—such a structure could take years to complete. So, he turned to the legends.

He left an offering beneath the great kukui tree.

And the Menehune had answered.

Through the night, the tiny builders labored, never pausing, never speaking. Stones were lifted as if weightless, walls rose as if conjured from the earth itself. The water shimmered, bending to their will.

The Menehune had only one rule: their work must never be seen by human eyes.

And so, as the sky paled to the first whispers of dawn, they vanished, their small feet making no sound, their presence erased by the rising sun.

But in their place, the fishpond stood—perfect, immovable, as if it had always been there.

A miracle.

Or perhaps, something more.

THE MYSTERY OF THE MENEHUNE – MYTH OR MEMORY?

The Menehune are among the most beloved and enduring figures in Hawaiian mythology. Described as a race of small but incredibly skilled craftsmen, their legends tell of impossible feats—entire temples, walls, and fishponds built in a single night, without a sound, without a trace of their presence left behind.

But could there be more to the story?

Hawaiian oral traditions speak of a people who lived in the islands long before the Polynesian settlers arrived. These early inhabitants, sometimes called the

Manahune in historical texts, were thought to be a smaller-statured people who lived in the deep forests and valleys, avoiding contact with the newcomers. Some historians speculate that these early Hawaiians may have been the real "Menehune"—skilled engineers and craftsmen who were gradually displaced by later settlers, their existence fading into legend.

Archaeological evidence supports this idea. The Menehune Fishpond on Kauaʻi, an ancient engineering marvel, is said to have been constructed overnight by the Menehune. Yet, its precision and scale suggest the work of highly skilled builders—perhaps an older, forgotten civilization whose knowledge has been lost to time.

Could the legends of the Menehune be whispers of a real people, their history buried beneath the weight of myth?

Or were they always, as the stories say, something more—something beyond human?

THE BUILDERS OF LEGENDS – CULTURAL SIGNIFICANCE

The legend of the Menehune is not just a tale of magic—it is a reflection of the values that shaped Hawaiian culture.

Hawaiians saw the Menehune as symbols of craftsmanship, intelligence, and the sacred duty of creating for the good of the land and its people. Their work, whether real or imagined, represented the highest ideals of ingenuity and hard work.

Even today, their name lingers in place names across the islands—Menehune Ditch, Menehune Fishpond, Menehune Road. Their story is woven into Hawaiian identity, a testament to the belief that greatness does not come from size, but from skill, dedication, and heart.

In a way, the Menehune never truly left.

They live on in the hands of modern Hawaiian artisans, in the stone walls that still stand, in the whispers of the wind through the valleys they once called home.

A REFLECTION ON MYTH, MEMORY, AND LEGACY

The story of the Menehune is not just about the past. It is about how we remember.

Every culture has its builders of legend—beings who shape the land, whose work defies time, whose existence hovers between history and myth. The Menehune remind us that not everything needs to be explained to be meaningful, that some mysteries are meant to be preserved, not solved.

Perhaps they were real. Perhaps they were never meant to be.

But in the quiet of the night, when the stars burn bright and the valleys grow silent, one cannot help but wonder:

What if they are still here?

Watching.

Waiting.

Building the impossible, just beyond the reach of human eyes.

CLOSING THOUGHT

"Some stories are not meant to be understood. Some are meant to remind us that wonder still exists, hidden in the corners of the world where the hands of legends once worked."

5

LOVE, BETRAYAL, AND THE WRATH OF THE GODS

"Some loves burn too brightly for this world. Some loves are torn apart by forces beyond mortal control. But the truest love—like the roots of the ʻŌhiʻa tree—endures, even beyond death."

The tragic love of ʻōhiʻa and lehua

The wind carried the scent of rain over the mountains, rustling the leaves of the great trees. The land was alive with color, but none so striking as the crimson blossoms of the lehua. They swayed in the breeze, delicate yet unbreakable, clinging to the sturdy branches of the ʻŌhiʻa tree.

Their love had not always been this way—silent, unmoving, bound by earth and root.

Once, ʻŌhiʻa had been a man. Strong, noble, and kind, his heart belonged to Lehua, the most beautiful woman in the village. Their love was pure, a devotion so deep that even the gods took notice.

And one god, in particular, did not approve.

Pele, the goddess of fire and volcanoes, watched ʻŌhiʻa with longing. She saw his strength, his unwavering spirit, and desired him for herself. But when she approached him, flames dancing in her eyes, ʻŌhiʻa did not waver.

"My heart belongs to Lehua," he said.

Pele's rage was swift and terrible.

If she could not have him, then no one would.

With a whisper of divine power, she cursed him—his body stiffening, his limbs twisting, his skin roughening into bark. Before Lehua's horrified eyes, the man she loved was no more. In his place stood a gnarled, lonely tree.

Lehua fell to her knees, her cries shaking the heavens. The other gods, moved by her sorrow, took pity on her. They could not undo Pele's curse, but they could grant her one mercy.

They transformed Lehua into a flower—delicate, crimson, clinging to the branches of the ʻŌhiʻa tree, so that even in death, she would never be apart from him.

But there was one final cruelty.

Whenever the lehua flower is plucked from the tree, the skies weep.

Even today, Hawaiians say that when rain falls suddenly from a clear sky, it is the sorrow of ʻŌhiʻa and Lehua—their love torn apart, their souls forever yearning.

LOVE, BETRAYAL, AND DIVINE WRATH IN HAWAIIAN MYTHOLOGY

Hawaiian mythology is filled with stories of love, passion, and devastating betrayal. Unlike the idealized romances of some cultures, these tales often come with warnings—about the power of the gods, the cost of defiance, and the inescapable consequences of fate.

The gods were not distant beings, removed from the lives of mortals. They walked among them, fell in love with them, and, at times, destroyed them.

Take the story of Hina and the Moon—Hina, a woman of great beauty and wisdom, grew tired of the mortal world and sought refuge in the heavens. She ascended to the moon, seeking peace, but in doing so, she left behind those who loved her. Some say she became lonely, forever gazing down at the world she abandoned.

Or consider Naupaka, the princess who fell in love with a commoner. Forbidden to be together, they were separated—Naupaka forced to live in the mountains, her lover bound to the sea. To this day, the naupaka flower blooms in halves, one in the mountains, the other by the ocean, forever apart.

These stories are more than myths; they are lessons. They teach reverence for the gods, caution in matters of the heart, and the understanding that not all love stories end in happiness.

THE 'ŌHI'A LEHUA TREE – SYMBOLISM AND CULTURAL SIGNIFICANCE

The legend of 'Ōhi'a and Lehua is not merely a tale of love lost—it is woven into the very fabric of Hawaiian culture. The 'Ōhi'a lehua tree is one of the first to grow on new lava fields, its roots taking hold in the barren, black rock, bringing life to what was once only fire and destruction.

It is a tree of resilience, a symbol of how love and life endure even in the harshest conditions.

Hawaiians hold great respect for the 'Ōhi'a tree, and its blossoms are used in sacred ceremonies and hula performances. But the legend remains a warning as well—picking a lehua flower may anger the spirits, bringing rain as a sign of their sorrow.

Even today, hikers in Hawaii pause before taking a lehua blossom. Some refuse to pick them at all.

Because some stories are not meant to be tested.

LOVE'S ENDURANCE – A REFLECTION ON THE TIMELESSNESS OF MYTH

What is it about tragic love stories that endure?

Perhaps it is because they remind us of love's true nature—not just joy, but sacrifice. Not just passion, but pain. True love is not about possession but devotion, even in separation, even in death.

ʻŌhiʻa and Lehua may no longer walk among us, but their story is written in the forests of Hawaii, in the red blossoms swaying in the wind, in the sudden rains that fall like tears.

Their love was tested by the gods. It was broken by divine jealousy.

And yet, it endures.

Like the roots of the ʻŌhiʻa tree, burrowing into ancient lava, holding fast against time itself.

CLOSING THOUGHT

"Some loves never fade, even when turned to stone and petals. Some loves remain, whispering in the wind, blooming with every sunrise, mourning with every rain."

6

THE MOʻO – GUARDIANS OF WATER AND SHADOW

"In the stillness of ancient waters, where moonlight shimmers upon black stones, something watches. Silent. Waiting. The Moʻo are not mere myths—they are the breath of the land, the keepers of sacred waters, the shadows that never truly vanish."

the whisper of the water – an encounter with a moʻo

The jungle pulsed with life, thick with the scent of damp earth and the distant murmur of flowing water. A traveler, weary from the heat, followed a narrow path through towering ferns, drawn by the sound of a hidden spring.

Then—silence.

The traveler hesitated, sensing something unseen. A flicker of movement in the shadows. The air grew thick, electric with an ancient presence.

The pool shimmered, reflecting the full moon like a silver mirror. Dark stones framed its edges, slick with moss, ancient and unmoving. But there, just beneath the surface—was it a ripple? Or something more?

A pair of luminous, golden eyes blinked open in the depths.

A voice, neither male nor female, neither near nor far, whispered through the leaves:

"Leave this place... unless you offer respect."

The traveler, heart pounding, remembered the stories. The Moʻo were not to be taken lightly.

Hurriedly, they bowed, whispered a prayer, and placed an offering of ti leaves at the water's edge.

The jungle exhaled. The tension lifted. The pool stilled once more.

Some say the Moʻo are long gone. But those who listen—those who truly see—know better.

THE MOʻO – ANCIENT GUARDIANS OF WATER

The Moʻo are among the most enigmatic beings in Hawaiian mythology—powerful reptilian spirits that shape-shift between human, lizard, and spirit form. They are neither fully gods nor mere animals, but something in between—guardians, rulers, and keepers of the sacred waters that sustain life.

In their true form, Moʻo are said to be enormous, their black, glistening bodies stretching for many feet. They reside in freshwater pools, waterfalls, caves, and hidden springs, protecting the land's most precious resource.

To anger a Moʻo is to invite disaster.

Legends tell of chiefs who disrespected sacred waters and paid the price—droughts, floods, and even death. The Moʻo were not simply monsters to be feared; they were spirits that demanded respect, a reminder that water is life, and life must be honored.

Hawaiians once placed stone shrines near sacred springs, offering ti leaves and chants to appease these guardians. It was a way of maintaining balance, ensuring that water continued to flow, sustaining both the people and the land.

TALES OF THE MOʻO — THE BATTLE BETWEEN GODS AND SPIRITS

Many Moʻo were benevolent, protecting those who honored them. But some were vengeful, their wrath legendary.

One of the most famous Moʻo was Kihawahine, a powerful spirit who once lived on Maui. She was a protector, but also a fierce enforcer of sacred law. Those who dared to defile her waters would be swallowed by the very earth itself.

Another tale speaks of Kapukapu, a Moʻo who could take the form of a beautiful woman. She tested the hearts of men, rewarding those who showed kindness and punishing those who sought only greed and power.

But the most famous battle was between the Moʻo and Pele herself.

Pele, the goddess of fire, sought to claim all that lay in her path, including the sacred pools of the Moʻo. Many of these guardian spirits stood against her, only to be turned to stone by her flames. Even today, certain lava formations bear the shapes of great lizards, remnants of this ancient war between fire and water.

And yet, not all Moʻo were destroyed.

Some say they still linger, hidden in the deep places of the land.

MOʻO AND THE HAWAIIAN CONNECTION TO WATER

Why did the Hawaiians revere the Moʻo?

Because water was, and remains, the most precious resource in the islands.

Freshwater springs meant survival. A flowing river could sustain an entire village. A sacred pond could feed generations. To pollute or misuse water was not just an offense against nature—it was an offense against the divine.

The Moʻo embodied this understanding. They were not mere myths; they were symbols of a deep ecological truth:

Water is life. And life must be protected.

Even today, the legacy of the Moʻo can be felt. The careful management of water sources, the reverence for sacred springs, and the continued respect for the land all stem from these ancient beliefs.

Modern Hawaiians still tell stories of the Moʻo, not just as legends, but as reminders.

For those who forget—those who disrespect the land—may yet find themselves lost in the jungle, hearing the whisper of unseen eyes watching from the water's edge.

THE ETERNAL GUARDIANS – A REFLECTION ON BALANCE AND RESPECT

Are the Moʻo real?

Perhaps not in the way some might expect. But in another sense, they are as real as the rivers and the rain.

They remind us of something deeper—of the need for balance between humans and nature, of the respect required to live in harmony with the land.

In the age of climate change, water scarcity, and environmental destruction, the wisdom of the Moʻo is more relevant than ever.

They teach us that guardianship is not just the duty of spirits—it is the duty of all.

And so, the Moʻo remain.

Waiting.

Watching.

Ensuring that those who drink from the sacred waters remember the old ways.

Because those who forget... may one day hear the whisper of the jungle and see golden eyes watching from the deep.

CLOSING THOUGHT

"The Mo'o are not gone. They are in the waters that quench the land, in the rains that bless the fields, in the silence of caves where time stands still. Respect them, and they will bless you. Defy them, and you will learn why shadows never truly vanish."

7

THE FALL OF THE KAPU SYSTEM – WHEN GODS WERE SILENCED

"A single meal can change the course of history. A single act can shatter the foundation of a civilization. On that fateful night, when the king crossed the divide, the gods of old stood silent, and the world of Hawaii was never the same."

The night the old gods fell

The torches burned low, flickering against the night wind. The feast before them was rich—roast pig, sweet poi, the scent of fresh fish rising into the humid air. Drums pounded softly in the distance, their rhythm steady, ancient.

But tonight, something was different.

The men sat on one side, the women on the other, as it had always been. The kapu system—sacred laws decreed by the gods—prohibited men and women from eating together. It was an unbreakable rule, a divine order upheld for centuries.

And then, King Kamehameha II stood.

The young king, known as Liholiho, took a deep breath. His mother, Queen Kaʻahumanu, watched, her gaze steady, unreadable.

Then, with deliberate hands, he lifted a piece of roasted pig and placed it onto the women's side of the feast.

Gasps rippled through the gathering. Eyes widened in shock. Some recoiled, expecting immediate divine retribution.

The gods did not speak.

The sky did not darken.

The earth did not tremble.

Liholiho sat beside the women and ate.

In that moment, the sacred order of Hawaii shattered. The kapu system—centuries of religious law, power, and divine rule—had fallen.

And the world of the old gods was left in silence.

WHAT WAS THE KAPU SYSTEM?

To understand the weight of this act, one must understand the kapu system itself.

For centuries, the kapu system was more than law—it was the very framework of Hawaiian life. It dictated what could be done, when, where, and by whom. It structured society, defined power, and ensured the favor of the gods.

The kapu laws determined:

Who could eat certain foods (women were forbidden from eating pork, bananas, coconuts, and some types of fish).

Who could enter sacred sites.

When and how fishing, farming, and building could be done.

Who had the right to speak to or approach the aliʻi (chiefs).

Breaking kapu was not a simple crime—it was a transgression against the gods themselves. The punishment was often death, swift and merciless, carried out by the kahuna (priests) or warriors of the ruling aliʻi.

Kapu was power.

Kapu was control.

Kapu was fear.

And yet, as foreign ships arrived, as new ideas crept in, cracks began to form in this once-unshakable system.

WHY DID THE KAPU SYSTEM FALL?

Many believe that the fall of the kapu system was inevitable. The world was changing, and Hawaii stood at the crossroads of history.

Several key factors led to its collapse:

The Death of Kamehameha the Great

Kamehameha I was a warrior king, the unifier of the Hawaiian Islands. He had upheld the kapu system, using it to solidify his rule. But when he died in 1819, his son, Liholiho, inherited a kingdom in transition. The old king's death left a power vacuum—one that his wives, particularly Kaʻahumanu, sought to fill.

The Rise of Queen Kaʻahumanu

Kaʻahumanu, Kamehameha's favored wife, was a force unlike any Hawaii had seen. Ambitious and politically shrewd, she sought to reshape the kingdom. She understood that the kapu system restricted power, particularly for women, and she saw an opportunity to dismantle it.

She became an advisor to young Kamehameha II, encouraging him to break tradition—to eat with the women, to challenge the gods, to undo the sacred laws.

Foreign Influence and the Arrival of Christianity

By the early 1800s, foreigners had already begun altering Hawaiian society. Traders, whalers, and explorers brought new ideas—among them, the concept of Christianity.

Hawaiians saw that these foreigners lived without kapu. They ate as they pleased. They did not suffer divine wrath.

Missionaries had not yet fully arrived, but whispers of a different god—one that did not demand rigid kapu laws—began to spread.

The ali'i saw this.

And they began to wonder: If the foreigners could live without kapu… could Hawaiians?

THE AFTERMATH – A KINGDOM WITHOUT KAPU

Once Liholiho ate with the women, the kingdom could not turn back.

The temples—once sacred places of worship—were abandoned. The great wooden idols were thrown into the sea or burned. The priests, once the most powerful figures in Hawaiian society, found themselves without purpose.

Some Hawaiians resisted, believing the gods would punish them. A rebellion broke out, led by the chief Kekuaokalani, who sought to restore the kapu system. But his forces were defeated. The gods remained silent.

The kapu system was dead.

And in its place, a new order began to rise—one that would change Hawaii forever.

THE ARRIVAL OF CHRISTIANITY AND THE TRANSFORMATION OF HAWAII

Not long after the fall of kapu, the first Christian missionaries arrived in 1820.

To them, Hawaii was a land in need of salvation. The timing could not have been more perfect—Hawaiians had just abandoned their ancient religion, leaving a spiritual void. The missionaries filled it.

The gods of old were replaced with a new God.

The chiefs who once ruled by divine right found their power challenged by a new force—Western laws, education, and commerce.

Hawaii was changing.

The loss of kapu was not just the loss of religious law—it was the loss of an entire way of life. It marked the beginning of Hawaii's rapid transformation, leading to the rise of Western influence, the erosion of native governance, and ultimately, the annexation of Hawaii by the United States.

But was the fall of kapu a liberation? Or the first step toward cultural erosion?

Hawaiians today still debate this.

Some see it as the necessary evolution of a civilization. Others see it as the moment their gods were silenced.

THE STRUGGLE BETWEEN TRADITION AND CHANGE

History is never simple. The end of kapu was neither entirely good nor entirely bad—it was both.

It freed Hawaiians from rigid laws, yet it also marked the beginning of the loss of their sovereignty. It opened doors to new ideas, yet it also allowed foreign influence to take root.

The fall of kapu was not just about laws.

It was about power.

It was about faith.

It was about the identity of a people standing at the edge of the old world and the new.

And in that moment—on that night when King Kamehameha II lifted his hands and broke the sacred law—Hawaii stepped into an uncertain future.

The gods did not speak.

But perhaps, if one listens closely to the wind that rustles the palms and the waves that kiss the shore, their echoes remain.

CLOSING THOUGHT

"The gods are never truly silent. They live in the land, in the stories, in the breath of a people who refuse to forget. The kapu fell, but the spirit of Hawaii endures."

8

THE CURSE OF KAMEHAMEHA'S BONES

"He who controls the bones controls the mana. And so, they were hidden—not buried, not marked, not meant to be found. To seek them is to invite the wrath of the unseen."

The final journey of a king

The sky burned crimson as the sun sank into the Pacific. The towering cliffs of Hawaiʻi Island stood like silent sentinels, watching as a small group of men moved swiftly, carrying a burden heavier than any weapon of war.

Wrapped in layers of kapa cloth, bound by sacred chants, the body of King Kamehameha the Great was being taken to its final resting place. But unlike the tombs of pharaohs or the grand burial mounds of ancient rulers, there would be no monument, no marker—only secrecy, shadows, and a curse that would last for generations.

These men—trusted warriors known as na ʻili—were tasked with an unbreakable duty: to hide the king's remains where no man could ever disturb them. To fail was to invite death. To speak of the location was to bring down divine retribution.

As they disappeared into the mountains, their footsteps swallowed by the jungle, the world of men lost sight of Kamehameha forever.

And with his bones, so too vanished his mana—his sacred power.

THE POWER OF BONES – WHY KAMEHAMEHA'S IWI WERE HIDDEN

To understand why Kamehameha's burial was shrouded in secrecy, one must first understand the Hawaiian concept of mana.

Mana was not just strength—it was divine energy, the spiritual force that flowed through chiefs, warriors, and nature itself. The bones (iwi) of great chiefs were believed to contain immense mana, making them both a source of power and a potential threat if they fell into the wrong hands.

In ancient Hawaii, a chief's bones were never simply buried. They were hidden, often in places only a select few knew—caves, cliffs, underwater caverns. This was done to prevent enemies from seizing them, for possessing the iwi of a great leader could grant power beyond reckoning.

This practice was known as hūnā iwi—the sacred concealment of bones.

For Kamehameha the Great, the stakes were even higher. As the unifier of the Hawaiian Islands, his mana was unparalleled. His enemies, though defeated, still existed. If his bones were found, they could be used to curse his lineage or alter the fate of the islands.

Thus, his warriors sealed his remains in secrecy so profound that, to this day, no one has ever found them.

But the legend does not end there.

Because those who seek Kamehameha's bones are said to awaken something far more dangerous than lost history.

THE CURSE – WHEN THE DEAD ARE DISTURBED

Across Hawaii, stories are whispered of those who have tried to find Kamehameha's resting place—and the misfortunes that followed.

Some say that deep in the valleys of Kohala or among the treacherous cliffs of Mauna Kea, seekers have vanished, their bodies never recovered. Others speak of strange visions, unnatural accidents, and a sense of being watched—an unseen force warning them to turn back.

One of the most chilling stories comes from the early 20th century, when a group of researchers set out to uncover hidden burial caves believed to hold the remains of aliʻi (chiefs). As they descended into one cavern, their torches flickered and died. The air grew heavy, thick with an energy that pressed against their chests.

A voice—no, a presence—was said to have whispered in the darkness: Leave.

They fled, abandoning the expedition, and soon after, two of them fell mysteriously ill.

The caves were never explored again.

Coincidence? Or a warning from beyond?

Even today, many believe that disturbing sacred burial sites brings misfortune. Hawaiian elders (kūpuna) warn against seeking Kamehameha's iwi, for the power they hold is not meant for the living.

The king rests where he was meant to rest.

And some secrets are better left undisturbed.

WHERE IS KAMEHAMEHA'S TOMB? THE THEORIES

Despite the warnings, the search for Kamehameha's bones has never truly stopped. Over the years, countless theories have emerged about where his remains might be hidden.

Here are some of the most persistent:

1. The Caves of Kohala

Kamehameha was born in Kohala, on the northern tip of the Big Island. Some believe his bones were returned there, hidden in one of the many lava tubes or sea caves that dot the coastline. These caves, difficult to access and prone to collapse, provide the perfect natural hiding place.

2. Mauna Kea – The Sacred Mountain

Mauna Kea, the tallest mountain in the Pacific, has long been considered a place of spiritual power. Many aliʻi were buried there, and some believe Kamehameha's warriors carried his body to the highest peaks, where it remains hidden beneath the ancient lava flows.

3. The Royal Mausoleum (Mauna ʻAla)

In the 19th century, many of Hawaii's ruling chiefs were reinterred at the Royal Mausoleum in Honolulu. Some believe Kamehameha's remains were secretly moved there—but no evidence has ever been found.

4. A Watery Grave

A less common theory suggests that Kamehameha's bones were hidden beneath the ocean, placed in an underwater cave or sunken within a sacred fishpond. This would align with Hawaiian traditions of concealing iwi in places unreachable by ordinary men.

But no matter the theory, one truth remains:

No one has ever found them.

And perhaps, no one ever will.

THE LEGACY OF THE HIDDEN KING

The mystery of Kamehameha's bones is more than just a legend—it is a symbol.

It represents the loss of old Hawaii, the secrecy of a past that colonial forces sought to erase. It is a reminder that not all history can be uncovered, nor should it be.

Hawaiians today continue to honor their ancestors through respect for sacred places. Many believe that searching for Kamehameha's tomb is an act of desecration, a violation of kapu. Instead, they focus on preserving his legacy through stories, traditions, and the spirit of aloha ʻāina—love for the land.

And so, the king remains hidden.

Not lost.

Just beyond the reach of those who would seek to claim him.

THE FINAL WARNING – SHOULD THE BONES BE FOUND?

But what if one day, someone does find Kamehameha's remains?

Would his mana return to the people?

Or would the curse awaken, bringing misfortune to those who dared to disturb him?

Perhaps it is best to let the past rest.

For in the whispers of the wind and the crashing of the waves, Kamehameha's spirit still speaks.

And the unseen guardians of his bones are always watching.

CLOSING THOUGHT

"Some secrets are not meant to be uncovered. Some legacies are not written in stone, but in the hush of the ocean, the hush of the leaves, the hush of time itself. Kamehameha does not need a grave to be remembered—his spirit is woven into the land, forever untouchable."

9

THE HAWAIIAN RENAISSANCE – RECLAIMING LOST STORIES

"A language nearly silenced, a dance nearly forgotten, a history nearly erased. But like the waves against the shore, the stories of Hawaii could not be held back forever."

The first chant – a child awakens to a forgotten voice

The boy sat cross-legged on the woven mat, staring up at the elders before him. The sound that filled the air was unlike anything he had ever heard—not a song, not a prayer, but something deeper.

A mele oli—a Hawaiian chant.

The voice was raw, powerful, rising and falling like the ocean. It spoke of kings and gods, of warriors and lovers, of battles fought long before he was born. He did not understand all the words, but he felt them.

For the first time in his young life, he felt Hawaiian.

And for the first time, he realized what had been taken from him.

This was not just a chant.

This was a call to awaken.

THE SILENCE BEFORE THE STORM – HOW HAWAII NEARLY LOST ITS VOICE

To understand the Hawaiian Renaissance, we must first understand the near-death of Hawaiian culture.

For centuries, Hawaii had been a sovereign kingdom with its own language, customs, and a history passed down through hula, mele, and oral traditions. But by the mid-20th century, that history was on the brink of being lost.

The Suppression of the Hawaiian Language

In 1893, the Hawaiian monarchy was overthrown by American-backed forces.

In 1896, the Hawaiian language (ʻōlelo Hawaiʻi) was banned in schools, forcing children to speak only English.

By the 1960s, fewer than 2,000 native speakers remained, and Hawaiian was classified as an endangered language.

The Westernization of Hawaii

Hula, once a sacred storytelling art, had been reduced to a tourist attraction.

Ancient chants were replaced by commercialized music.

Hawaiian history was rewritten through a colonial lens, erasing or distorting native perspectives.

Hawaii was no longer telling its own story.

And so, the people forgot.

THE SPARK OF REVIVAL – THE HAWAIIAN RENAISSANCE BEGINS

In the 1970s, something changed.

A new generation of Hawaiians, raised without their native tongue, without their ancestral stories, began to ask questions. Who were they before America? Before plantations, before tourism, before statehood?

And more importantly—could they reclaim what was lost?

The answer was yes.

1. The Revival of the Hawaiian Language

In 1978, Hawaiian was re-established as an official state language.

Hawaiian language immersion schools (Nā Pūnana Leo) were created, teaching children the language once forbidden.

Universities introduced Hawaiian studies programs, ensuring future generations could study their own history.

What was once nearly extinct began to breathe again.

2. The Return of Hula – More Than Just a Dance

Traditional hula kahiko (ancient hula) was resurrected, returning to its spiritual and storytelling roots.

The Merrie Monarch Festival, a prestigious hula competition, grew in prominence, showcasing the deep cultural and historical significance of the dance.

Hula became a political act—a way of reclaiming identity and resisting assimilation.

3. The Fight for Sovereignty and Land Rights

The movement to recognize Hawaiian sovereignty gained momentum.

Native Hawaiians began to protest land mismanagement, advocating for the return of ancestral lands.

In 1976, the Hōkūleʻa, a traditional Polynesian voyaging canoe, set sail without modern instruments, proving that Hawaiians had navigated the Pacific long before Western explorers.

It was a statement to the world: Hawaiians were not passive victims of history. They were still here.

MYTHS RECLAIMED – LEGENDS AS A WEAPON OF IDENTITY

One of the most profound aspects of the Hawaiian Renaissance was the reclaiming of myths and legends.

For decades, Hawaiian mythology had been dismissed as mere folklore, stripped of its deeper meaning. But now, scholars, artists, and storytellers breathed new life into these ancient tales.

The story of Pele was no longer just a volcano myth—it was a symbol of resilience and the fiery spirit of the Hawaiian people.

The legend of Maui snaring the sun was no longer just a children's tale—it was a metaphor for Hawaiians taking back control of their own time, their own destiny.

The prophecy of Kamehameha the Great rising from the stars was no longer just history—it was a reminder that Hawaii had once been a kingdom, and perhaps, one day, it could be again.

Myths were no longer just stories.

They were resistance.

THE HAWAIIAN RENAISSANCE TODAY – HAS THE DREAM BEEN FULFILLED?

The Hawaiian Renaissance achieved many victories, but the struggle is far from over.

The Challenges:

Hawaii still faces economic and political pressures that threaten native traditions.

The cost of living forces many native Hawaiians to leave their homeland.

Tourism, while providing income, often commercializes and misrepresents Hawaiian culture.

But despite these challenges, the legacy of the Renaissance remains strong.

The Hawaiian language is growing once more, with thousands of fluent speakers.

Hula is respected as both an art and a sacred practice.

Hawaiian myths are told not just in books but in films, music, and global storytelling.

Most importantly, Hawaiians are telling their own stories again.

And as long as the stories live, so too does the soul of Hawaii.

THE FINAL WORD – WHAT THE RENAISSANCE MEANS FOR THE FUTURE

As the young boy on the mat listens to the chant, something stirs inside him.

A knowing. A connection.

He may not understand all the words yet, but he understands their meaning.

He belongs to something ancient, something powerful.

The past is not dead.

It is in the voice of the elder, the rhythm of the drum, the whisper of the wind through the taro fields.

It is in the myths that refuse to be forgotten.

The Hawaiian Renaissance was not just about reviving a culture.

It was about proving that culture had never truly died.

It had only been waiting.

Waiting for the moment when the people would remember who they were.

And now, they have.

CLOSING THOUGHT

"The land remembers. The ocean remembers. And the stories, long buried, rise again—like the tide, like the sun, like the people who will never be silenced."

10

THE TIMELESS ECHO OF LEGENDS

"The waves remember. The wind remembers. And through them, the voices of the ancients still speak."

The ocean whispers – a reflection on time and storytelling

The sea stretches endless before us, a shimmering expanse of memory and myth.

Beneath its rolling waves lie the echoes of a thousand voices—chants sung to the stars, prayers whispered to the gods, legends told beneath a canopy of fire-lit palms.

To some, the past is distant, a relic of another world.

But in Hawaii, the past is alive.

The gods still walk. The spirits still march. The tricksters still weave their mischief, and the ancestors still call upon the wind.

The legends never ended.

They simply wait for us to listen.

THE DIVINE HAND – THE MYTHS THAT SHAPED THE LAND

From the molten fury of Pele to the guiding hand of Maui, Hawaii's landscape is more than earth and stone. It is the imprint of gods.

The Birth of the Islands – Pele's fire still burns beneath the surface, her presence felt in every eruption.

Maui and the Sun – The demigod's cleverness still lingers in the balance of day and night, a reminder that even time itself can be shaped by will.

The Menehune's Hidden Work – Though unseen, their legacy stands in the stonework, the ponds, the ancient ruins left behind as whispers of a forgotten race.

The mountains and valleys are more than geography. They are stories made solid.

Every wave that crashes, every lava flow that carves new earth—it is not just nature.

It is the gods, still creating.

THE LESSONS OF HEROES AND TRICKSTERS – WISDOM IN THE TALES

Hawaiian myths are not mere entertainment. They are lessons, wrapped in the fabric of legend.

Maui's daring exploits teach us the power of wit and courage, the ability to challenge the impossible.

The tragic love of ʻŌhiʻa and Lehua reminds us of devotion, sacrifice, and the delicate balance of love and loss.

The fall of the Kapu system warns us that even the strongest traditions can crumble when the world begins to shift.

In every legend, a truth.

In every truth, a lesson for those who will listen.

THE POWER OF SPIRITS – WHEN THE PAST REFUSES TO SLEEP

Hawaii is a land where the veil between the living and the dead is thin.

The Night Marchers still roam, a warning to those who would disrespect the sacred.

The Moʻo, guardians of water, still whisper in the hidden pools, reminding us to honor the land that sustains us.

The bones of kings remain lost, their power lingering, their resting places untouched by time.

The past is never buried.

It moves, breathes, and watches.

To ignore it is to invite misfortune.

To honor it is to walk in harmony with the ancestors.

THE STRUGGLE TO REMEMBER – THE RENAISSANCE OF IDENTITY

For generations, these legends were silenced.

The language that carried them was banned. The dances that honored them were reduced to spectacle. The gods who ruled the land were forgotten, their temples left to ruin.

But as the Hawaiian Renaissance proved—no culture can be erased forever.

Through the resurgence of ʻōlelo Hawaiʻi, through the revival of hula, through the rediscovery of the myths that once guided an entire people, Hawaii remembered itself.

The legends were not lost.

They were only waiting.

MYTHS AS LIVING FORCES – THE FUTURE OF HAWAIIAN STORYTELLING

What, then, is the purpose of these stories today?

Are they merely echoes of a distant time? Or are they living, breathing forces that shape the present?

The answer is clear.

Pele's fire still reshapes the land, reminding us of nature's power and destruction.

The lessons of Maui still inspire innovation, teaching us to challenge limits and redefine what is possible.

The spirits of the ancestors still guide those who honor them, ensuring that the connection between past and present is never truly broken.

Myths are not static.

They evolve, grow, and find new voices in each generation.

They do not belong to the past.

They belong to those who carry them forward.

THE FINAL WORD – A LEGACY THAT WILL NEVER FADE

Some say myths are just stories.

But in Hawaii, myths are memory.

They are woven into the cliffs, carried by the tides, whispered by the wind.

They are written in the stars that guided voyagers across the Pacific.

They are sung in the chants that refuse to be silenced.

They are alive.

And as long as the waves kiss the shore, as long as the volcanoes breathe, as long as there are those who will listen—

The legends of Hawaii will never fade.

They will endure.

Just as they always have.

CLOSING THOUGHT

"A story never dies as long as someone remembers. And in Hawaii, the legends will always be remembered."

Made in the USA
Columbia, SC
10 July 2025